SO-CTA-576

The GREAT Rex

by Tanner Gay

illustrations by Len Ebert

Harcourt Brace & Company

Orlando   Atlanta   Austin   Boston   San Francisco   Chicago   Dallas   New York   Toronto   London

Have you met The Great Rex? Well, let me tell you—Rex is the best!

"Come one, come all!" yell
the men who sell the show. "See
what The Great Rex gets into!
See how he gets out!"

The men help Rex get into a
keg. "All set?" yell the men.
"You bet!" yells Rex.

The men put the keg down
into a well. Will Rex get out?

Yes! Up comes Rex, wet but laughing! The people yell, "Rex is the best!"

Rex sees Pretty Nell. Nell is always there to wish Rex well.

Next, the men help Rex get into a net. "All set?" yell the men.

"You bet!" yells Rex.

The men put Rex and the net
down into a den. Will Rex get
out?

Yes! Out comes Rex, full of
pep! "Rex is the best!" yell the
people.

10

Rex looks around. Pretty Nell
is there to wish Rex well.

Rex gets into a pen up to his neck! "All set?" yell the men. "You bet!" yells Rex.

Next, the pen is set on the
end of a deck. In Rex goes! Will
he get out?

Yes! Out comes Rex, like a jet!
"Rex is the best!" yell the
people.

"Thank you!" says Rex. "The best is yet to come! I beg you to come back in ten days."

Why?

Because in ten days, Rex and
Nell will be wed. All the people
will come to wish them well!

Teacher/Family Member

Ask children to name two or three things from which The Great
Rex escaped (keg, well, net, den, pen). Discuss how the words
are alike (same vowel sound). Then have children choose two of
the words and make a list of rhyming words for each.

Phonics Reinforced in This Book

Phonic Element: Short vowel: /e/e

Decodable Words with the Phonic Element: *met, Rex, well, let, tell,
best, yell, men, sell, help, get(s), red, keg, set, bet, yells, yes, wet,
Nell, next, net, den, pep, pen, neck, led, end, deck, jet, yet, beg,
ten, wed*

Phonograms with the Phonic Element: *-et, -ell, -en, -ed, -eck, -eg*

Target High-Frequency Words: *great, a, always, because, come, people,
see, show*

Word Count: 243

Copyright © by Harcourt Brace & Company

All rights reserved. No part of this publication may be reproduced or transmitted in any form or by any means,
electronic or mechanical, including photocopy, recording, or any information storage and retrieval system, without
permission in writing from the publisher.

Requests for permission to make copies of any part of the work should be mailed to: Permissions Department,
Harcourt Brace & Company, 6277 Sea Harbor Drive, Orlando, FL 32887-6777.

HARCOURT BRACE and Quill Design is a registered trademark of Harcourt Brace & Company.

Printed in the United States of America

ISBN 0-15-308983-0

Ordering Options
ISBN 0-15-309427-3 (Package of 5)
ISBN 0-15-309072-3 (Grade 3 Package)
ISBN 0-15-309255-6 (Grade 3 Package with Display Box and Teacher's Guide)

5 6 7 8 9 10 974 00

BOOK **2**

Phonics

PRACTICE
READERS

3-1

0-15-308983-0

90000 >

9 780153 089831

HARCOURT
BRACE

SOCCER TALK

By Marilyn Sherman